First-Class
Stamp Here

Dear

I am

Please support

This matters to me because

Sincerely,

My address:

My Elected Officials

Name:_____ Office held:_____
Address:_____
City:_____ State:_____ Zip code:_____
Phone:_____
E-mail:_____

Name:_____ Office held:_____
Address:_____
City:_____ State:_____ Zip code:_____
Phone:_____
E-mail:_____

Name:_____ Office held:_____
Address:_____
City:_____ State:_____ Zip code:_____
Phone:_____
E-mail:_____

Name:_____ Office held:_____
Address:_____
City:_____ State:_____ Zip code:_____
Phone:_____
E-mail:_____

Name:_____ Office held:_____
Address:_____
City:_____ State:_____ Zip code:_____
Phone:_____
E-mail:_____

your note. If you're writing about a piece of legislation, refer to it by its full name.

- **Include specific details and personal stories.** If applicable, support your points with facts and data (and be sure to cite your sources). You can also make your message memorable by sharing how an issue personally affects you, your family, or your community.

- **Keep your message brief.** Offices, especially congressional ones, can receive hundreds of letters each day. Make things easier for your elected officials and their staffers with a concise message. Paragraphs are a tried and true way to convey your thoughts, but a bulleted list is also an efficient format for sharing information, especially if you're citing data.

- **Be respectful.** Simple things such as using a proper salutation (e.g., the Honorable . . ., Senator . . ., etc.) and ending your note with a "thank you for your time" can make a difference. A message that politely outlines why you disagree with a course of action will always be more persuasive than one full of angry words, profanity, or personal insults. Never threaten your representatives—this could get you into big trouble.

- **Write to your officials, even if you support their views.** Let your government leaders know when they're doing a great job and thank them for their work. Encouraging notes are not only wonderful to read, they also let your representatives know that they should continue their current course of action. It's also an opportunity to tell them what you'd like them to do next.

- **Make postcard writing a group activity.** Writing to your elected officials doesn't have to be a solo activity. Plus, when you have many people writing about the same issue, it makes it harder for your elected official to ignore. Invite your friends and family to join you or organize a meeting with your favorite community group.

Introduction

*Congress shall make no law respecting an establishment of religion,
or prohibiting the free exercise thereof; or abridging the freedom
of speech, or of the press; or the right of the people peaceably to
assemble, and to petition the Government for a redress of grievances.*
—First Amendment, The Constitution of the United States

The ability to write to our government leaders, whether they are members of Congress or your local school board, is a time-honored tradition. Each year, millions of letters addressed to our elected officials wind their way through the United States postal system. In fact, putting a pen to paper is one of the most effective ways to talk about the issues that matter to you.

Compared to the immediacy of a telephone call or e-mail, the humble postcard is a slower way to share what's on your mind, but what it lacks in speed, it makes up for in impact. A carefully crafted message signals thoughtfulness—plus, the constituent who takes the time to craft a meaningful message will often also take the time to vote. A message might call attention to an issue or express a popular opinion that a representative might not have been aware of before. It provides a written, easy-to-track record of how your government leaders can better serve you and your community. With just a pen, a stamp, and a postcard, it's easy to start taking action and making a difference.

A Postcard Writing Primer

What's the best way of getting an official's attention? How much should I write? Who's reading these things anyway? There's a lot to keep in mind when you want to write an effective letter. The postcards in this book provide four different templates that will help you outline your message, but if you're looking for more information to get started, here's a list of some helpful tips.

- **Determine the best person to write to.** Are you worried about a piece of legislation passing through Congress, or are you focused more on the local level? While the members of Congress influence national policy, the officials working in your town, state, or county government also have a huge impact on your day-to-day life. They might be better suited to handling certain concerns, and in the case of local government offices with fewer constituents, they might be able to give your message more personalized attention. To learn who your elected officials are and how you can get in touch, visit **usa.gov/elected-officials**. The websites for your state, county, or local government are also excellent resources for contact information.

- **Know who your readers are.** For legislators with many constituents, such as congressional representatives, most letters are often read by staffers, who record their contents and compile them into briefings. For local government offices, your first reader might be the official that you're contacting. Rest assured, no matter who is reviewing your postcards, your readers will consider your message carefully.

- **Introduce yourself and include your zip code.** Are you a parent? A member of a community organization? Do you work in an industry that is affected by a proposed bill or policy? Do you have expertise on a particular issue? Provide a brief bio, list your credentials, or mention if you're writing on behalf of an organization, especially if this information is pertinent to the issue you're addressing. You can also include your full address, but leaving at least a zip code is essential. It lets your reader know whether you live in a legislator's district. In fact, some offices might screen specifically for messages from constituents.

- **Be specific and recommend a course of action.** The most effective messages focus on one issue and state their purpose simply and clearly. This makes it easy for letter readers to correctly catalog

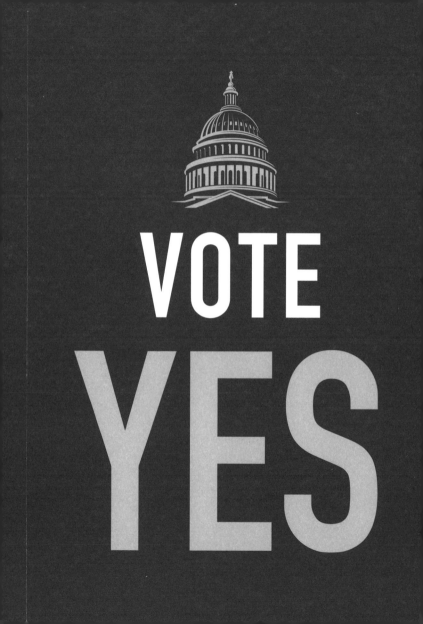

First-Class
Stamp Here

Dear

I am

Please support

This matters to me because

Sincerely,

My address:

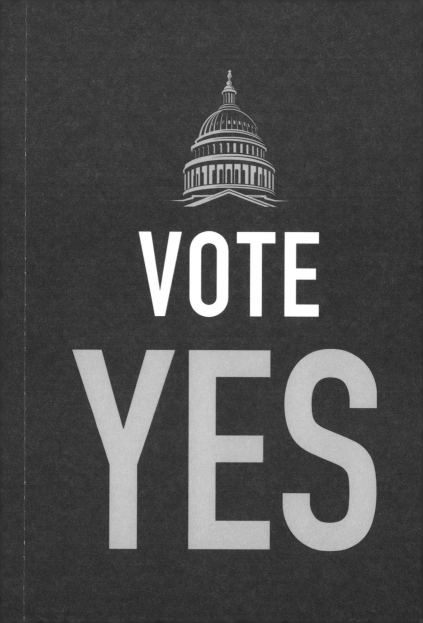

First-Class
Stamp Here

Dear

I am

Please support

This matters to me because

Sincerely,

My address:

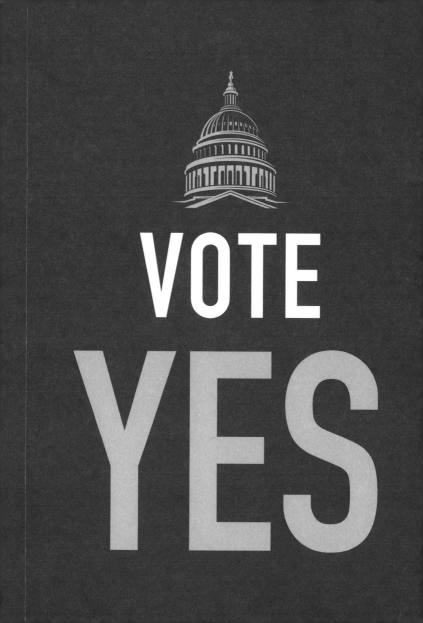

Dear

I am

Please support

This matters to me because

Sincerely,

My address:

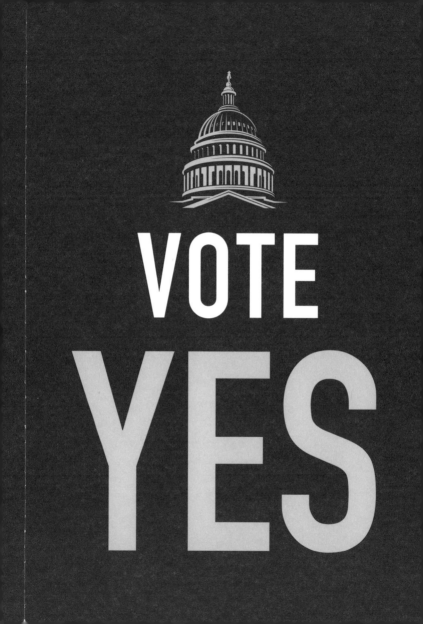

Dear

I am

Please support

This matters to me because

Sincerely,

My address:

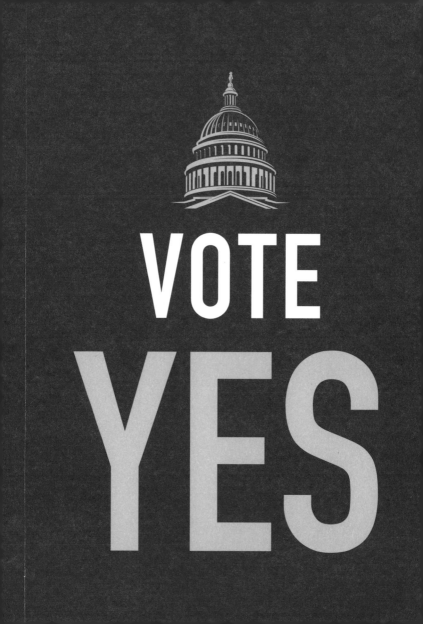

First-Class
Stamp Here

Dear

I am

Please support

This matters to me because

Sincerely,

My address:

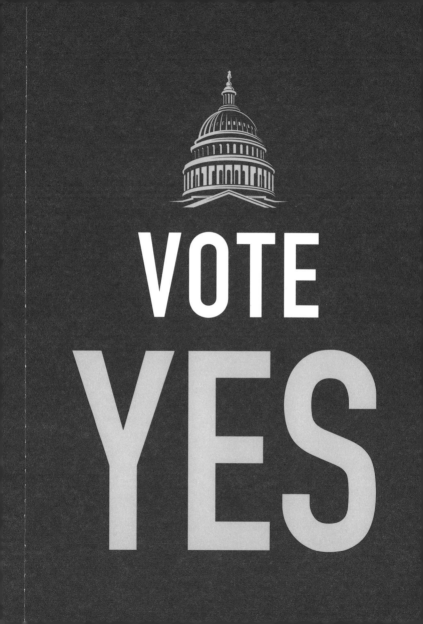

First-Class
Stamp Here

Dear

I am

Please support

This matters to me because

Sincerely,

My address:

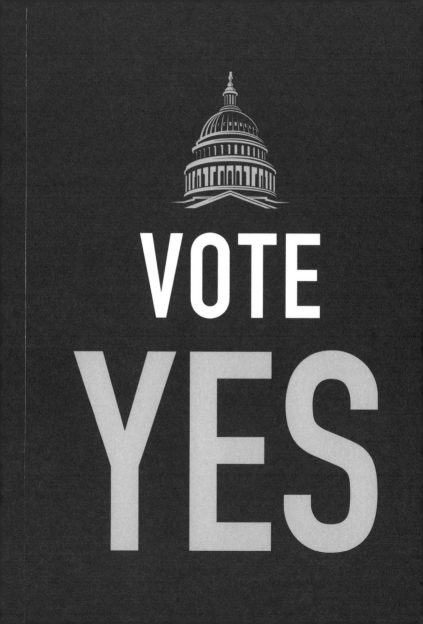

First-Class
Stamp Here

Dear

I am

Please support

This matters to me because

Sincerely,

My address:

Dear

I am

Please support

This matters to me because

Sincerely,

My address:

First-Class
Stamp Here

Dear

I am

Please oppose

This matters to me because

Sincerely,

My address:

First-Class
Stamp Here

Dear

I am

Please oppose

This matters to me because

Sincerely,

My address:

First-Class
Stamp Here

Dear

I am

Please oppose

This matters to me because

Sincerely,

My address:

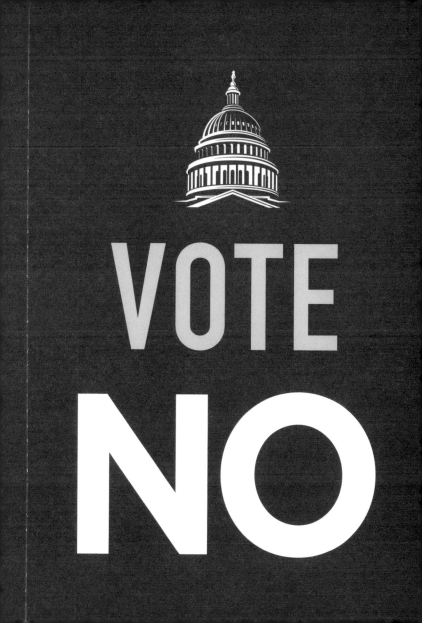

First-Class
Stamp Here

Dear

I am

Please oppose

This matters to me because

Sincerely,

My address:

First-Class
Stamp Here

Dear

I am

Please oppose

This matters to me because

Sincerely,

My address:

Dear

I am

Please oppose

This matters to me because

Sincerely,

My address:

First-Class
Stamp Here

Dear

I am

Please oppose

This matters to me because

Sincerely,

My address:

First-Class
Stamp Here

Dear

I am

Please oppose

This matters to me because

Sincerely,

My address:

First-Class
Stamp Here

Dear

I am

Please oppose

This matters to me because

Sincerely,

My address:

First-Class
Stamp Here

Dear

I am

Thank you for

I hope that you

Sincerely,

My address:

First-Class
Stamp Here

Dear

I am

Thank you for

I hope that you

Sincerely,

My address:

First-Class
Stamp Here

Dear

I am

Thank you for

I hope that you

Sincerely,

My address:

Dear

I am

Thank you for

I hope that you

Sincerely,

Dear

I am

Thank you for

I hope that you

Sincerely,

My address:

First-Class
Stamp Here

Dear

I am

Thank you for

I hope that you

Sincerely,

My address:

First-Class Stamp Here

Dear

I am

Thank you for

I hope that you

Sincerely,

My address:

Dear

I am

Thank you for

I hope that you

Sincerely,

My address:

First-Class
Stamp Here

Dear

I am

Thank you for

I hope that you

Sincerely,

My address:

First-Class
Stamp Here

Dear

I am

I'm writing to ask

This matters to me because

Sincerely,

My address:

First-Class
Stamp Here

Dear

I am

I'm writing to ask

This matters to me because

Sincerely,

My address:

First-Class
Stamp Here

Dear

I am

I'm writing to ask

This matters to me because

Sincerely,

My address:

First-Class
Stamp Here

Dear

I am

I'm writing to ask

This matters to me because

Sincerely,

My address:

First-Class
Stamp Here

Dear

I am

I'm writing to ask

This matters to me because

Sincerely,

My address:

First-Class
Stamp Here

Dear

I am

I'm writing to ask

This matters to me because

Sincerely,

My address:

Dear

I am

I'm writing to ask

This matters to me because

Sincerely,

My address:

First-Class
Stamp Here

Dear

I am

I'm writing to ask

This matters to me because

Sincerely,

My address:

Dear

I am

I'm writing to ask

This matters to me because

Sincerely,

My address:

Dear

I am

I'm writing to ask

This matters to me because

Sincerely,

My address:

First-Class
Stamp Here

Dear

I am

I'm writing to ask

This matters to me because

Sincerely,

My address:

Dear

I am

I'm writing to ask

This matters to me because

Sincerely,

My address:

STERLING
New York

An Imprint of Sterling Publishing Co., Inc.
1166 Avenue of the Americas
New York, NY 10036

ISBN 978-1-4549-2842-3

Distributed in Canada by Sterling Publishing Co., Inc.
c/o Canadian Manda Group, 664 Annette Street
Toronto, Ontario, Canada M6S 2C8
Distributed in the United Kingdom by GMC Distribution Services
Castle Place, 166 High Street, Lewes, East Sussex, England BN7 1XU
Distributed in Australia by NewSouth Books
45 Beach Street, Coogee, NSW 2034, Australia

For information about custom editions, special sales, and premium
and corporate purchases, please contact Sterling Special Sales at
800-805-5489 or specialsales@sterlingpublishing.com.

Manufactured in Canada

2 4 6 8 10 9 7 5 3 1

sterlingpublishing.com

Design by Igor Satanovsky
U.S. Capitol dome illustration: Alexkava/Shutterstock
Megaphone icon: Miraga Niftali/Shutterstock

POLITICAL SCIENCE/Civics & Citizenship

$9.95 U.S. / $11.95 CAN.

We all have something to say about our nation's political issues—so speak out, with these 40 postcards, plus tips for writing to your elected officials. Craft an impactful message using one of the four fill-in prompts printed on each card: there's one for opposing a policy, another for supporting one, and others to say "thank you" or to urge your representatives to take action on a cause that matters to you. Whatever your point of view, this postcard book makes it easy to share what's on your mind.

★★

ISBN 978-1-4549-2842-3

STERLING
New York

Manufactured in Canada